FACTS

Facts

BRUCE TAYLOR

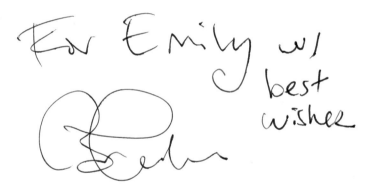

For Emily w/
best
wishes

SIGNAL
EDITIONS

SIGNAL EDITIONS IS AN IMPRINT OF VÉHICULE PRESS

ACKNOWLEDGEMENTS

Some of these poems appeared first in *Books in Canada*,
Index, and *Prism International*.

Thanks to Richard Sanger and Robyn Sarah

Véhicule Press acknowledges the support of
The Canada Council for the Arts for its publishing program.

Signal Editions editor: Michael Harris
Cover art and design by J.W. Stewart
Cover imaging by André Jacob
Typeset in Perpetua by Simon Garamond
Printed by AGMV-Marquis Inc.

CANADIAN CATALOGUING IN PUBLICATION

Taylor, Bruce, 1960-
Facts

Poems.
ISBN 1-55065-104-8

I. Title.

PS8589.A8816F32 1998   C811'.54   C98-901114-3
PR9199.3.T355F32 1998

Published by Véhicule Press
P.O.B. 125, PLACE DU PARC STATION
MONTRÉAL, QUÉBEC H2W 2M9

http://www.cam.org/~vpress

Distributed by General Distribution Services

Printed in Canada on alkaline paper.

CONTENTS

DOODLE

I have doodled a fantastic picture,
definitely worth keeping.
But what does it mean?
It shows a man in black pajamas sleeping
in a black gelatinous machine.
He is a lunatic, I think.
He dreams of piloting a submarine
in latitudes of permanent black ink
through oceans of condensed malarkey,
spirals, hieroglyphics, grids,
corkscrews, checkerboards and pyramids.
But he is not himself at all.
His mind feels funny being fondled by
that Muse of Incoherence who reclines
above him on a cloud of wavy lines,
jumbling the objects in his sky.
Chinese letters and occult designs.
What could any of it signify?
That ink is shallow, and yet deep.
That meanings mate and multiply,
tousling the air above our sleep.
That q resembles p, as x does y.

Or something else. But what? The truth
is tortuous, you'd be surprised.
This drowsy harlequin materialized
while I was on the telephone arranging
for a cheque I'd written not to bounce.
I had some funds transferred between accounts,
and as my ghostly treasures were exchanging
values in the hidden vaults
of the magnetic storage-chambers where
the ciphers of my hedonism waltz,
this thing began appearing in a corner
of a page of my agenda and

inexorably snuck across the paper,
self-engendered, eerily unplanned,
like Escher's famous drawing of a hand
that draws a hand that draws another hand.

It happens quietly, without commotion.
Your mind is elsewhere. Something interferes
with empty paper and a thing appears:
a madman on a jewelled ocean.
And that is what my poem wants as well,
to make things happen, but without exertion—
baffling arabesques unfurled
like faxes from the underworld
in one authoritative motion.

It needs the fluency and expertise
of the ingenious, brainless world,
which doodles on itself incessantly,
scribbling meanders on the parched plateaus,
Moroccan carpets on a reptile's back,
black veins in the pliations of a rose,
medieval riddles in a woodworm's track.
The world is lavish, never at a loss.
It puts a caterpillar in a ball of string,
then dresses it in oriental cloth—
batik for the monarch's wing,
paisley for the moth.

It does all that without a plan,
lacquering the beetle's shell,
kinking the horns of the gazelle,
composing tracts of timeless nonsense
in the cursive of the runner bean.
Does anyone who sits beneath a willow
know what its gesticulations mean?
The speechless bulk of the created world
is made entirely out of marginalia,
weird caprices that assail

the central tissues. Oh, to fill the pale
middle of my life with frail
finials and diaphanous rosettes
and have a heart as pink and ruffled
and confused as an azalea!

MARCH 1

Sometime today I'm turning 35.
The cover of Time would like to know
"When did the Universe Begin?"
God would tell us if he were alive.

If God were alive I'd tell him where to go.
I guess I'd go to Maui if I could,
get away from all this fucking snow.
I think Hawaiians make their gods from wood,

a friend of mine has got one on a shelf.
I'd find it strange to get down on my knees
in front of something that I'd carved myself.
Skip a step, perhaps, and worship trees.

The universe has been in style this year,
you run across it in the magazines.
No one wonders why the thing is here
or whether it will end in smithereens,

but when, exactly, did it first appear.
I gather it's unfolding. Earlier today,
my mother called me on the phone to say
I'd used up half of my "allotted span."

How long since whoever made it first began
decanting eons from the crystal flask?
You wouldn't think a magazine called "Time"
would have to ask.

TOMATO HORNWORM

At what age did I learn that life
was something you could fail at?
That a life conducted badly leads
to rooms with blankets on the windows,
suppers of hard-boiled eggs,
a townhouse hunched between the legs
of an electric pylon. Bingo dabbers.
Pants that won't stay up.
Years spent poking at a screen,
dislodging molecules of fun.

When I hear hailstones rattle on a skylight,
watch a red bug climbing up a stem,
or admire a Nile-shaped crack in my wall,
in what sense am I living well?

How many times must I have liked the wine
before I can honestly say
What years those were,
if only I had them back?

If three times in five the wine is astringent,
the blubber discoloured,
the eggs a bit off,
then in some sense I must have done this
wrongly, ruined a good life
with crummy selections, botched
my self-portrait
with unstable paints and a varnish
that everyone knew would turn black.

Now something is slowly moving across its life,
a tomato hornworm .
It seems to care which way it goes,
it wants to live well,
it appears not to know
how horrid it is no matter what it does.

FRESCO BLUE

Fresco blue, you could say, the blue of a saint's frock,
the sky over these boats so clear it hurts to stare.
The boats rising and falling on small waves.

A shocking emptiness. Like flares in the lens.
Not one ledge for an angel to perch on,
not one thin wire to hang a bird.

Not enough.

That isn't the sky I thought up on my own,
where gulls in cottony gowns go flying
and the clouds in their judicial wigs
unroll charters and certificates.
There is not much to look up to up there.
I think it would scare me
if I weren't used to it.

It is strange to have no plans.
Only this morning I had wanted to write a long book.

AS FOR THE BRAIN

As for the brain, it does not regenerate.
Its cells are dying every day.
It is dissolving at a certain rate
and little birds are taking it away.
How many painless decades of decay
can it look forward to before
there is too little of it left to say
"I love my yellow sweater," or
"By God, this food tastes great"?

It ends more slowly than it starts
(assuming you're not flattened by a car).
One by one you lose your moving parts
while gradually forgetting who you are.
In time, or out of it, you die.
There is no rapture, no impartial eye,
no land of shadows, no celestial dance,
no watchful, gentle, supernatural guy
who gives expended selves a second chance.
You are not reborn as an immortal
astral blur, diaphanous, unsexed,
to loiter at the phosphorescent portal
in between this kingdom and the next.
You do not waft above familiar ground,
or fondle dark-eyed lovers in a dream
or seize familiar objects with a hand
as insubstantial as a flashlight beam.
Thought stops. Distillates of what you were
quietly infiltrate the aquifer.

Experts on the afterlife will say
that if you had been able to obey
a few small maxims (as you *were* instructed)
in the end you might have been conducted
to a country where the rivers flow

with liquid invert sugar and pink lemonade
and nothing rhymes with breath. But as you know
we poets are extravagantly paid
to tell the truth. The truth is that we go,
one by one beneath the clumpy dirt,
the spirit unwilling but the flesh inert.

As for the brain, it hates this, but it spends
the only life it has designing boots,
or stencilling the eyebrows on a doll,
or pressing grout between ceramic tiles.
It throws some paper in a waterfall.
Somewhere inside itself it smiles.

THE SLOUGH

Are the entrails clear, immaculate cabbage?
—Theodore Roethke, "Unfold! Unfold!"

What's under the pudding skin, down in the slough
where the weed-pods root whose heads poke through
to goggle and bob in their seedy hats,
pithless and punch-drunk, chewed by gnats,
knocked flat by a damp, disagreeable breeze,
gusts of bad weather, abrupt as a sneeze
and stilt-birds sunk to their bamboo knees
in whatever is under the slough?

What's under the mud that schmecks our boots?
A raft of bedsprings lashed with roots,
spavined lumber, cans of glue,
electrical cables, lampreys, newts,
and, if what the neighbours say is true,
the ribs of a horse that once fell through
while pursuing a dog, who's in there too:
so all poor beasts that flit or thud
lie down with the frogs in the lathered mud,
who mate in the ruts where the tractor treads,
spin their milky, gelatinous threads
of spunk and spittle and clean, green eggs
that hatch like bean-sprouts, sprout hind legs
and rise, scientifically, out of the ooze
to walk upright in soft-soled shoes
and ponder the matter of what or who's
in the slough.

Off in the aftermath, what's up there?
A million metric tons of air.
Peacocks in the weeping figs
amble through a land of twigs
and flocks of phosphorescent, screaming

crook-nosed parrots copulate
upside down inside the gleaming
spirals of an iron gate.
Plying the trackless, gassy skies,
the wild cranes have crazy eyes
and jagged claws and skinny necks.
The natural world is quite complex.
Praising nature, one suspects
the Lombardy poplars pitch and sway
because these trees are having sex
with other trees three miles away.
Help me Ted, my days are dense
with moments that do not make sense!
Where is the love that spins the gears,
that honks the goose and flaps the crane
and cranks the sun and other stars
across the crinkled diaphane?
Where is the foot that pumps the treadle?
Whose the hand that tracks the moth?
Who scales the wooden frame of evening
tacking bolts of yellow cloth?
Who ignores this? When is ever?
Why am I stupid? What is true?
None of that transmutes to answers
anywhere next to, beneath, or on top of,
over or under the slough.

AND BLACKBIRDS

When I was quite young and easy to amaze
I stared at the word AND on a billboard,
and I seemed to see down
through its surface of paper and nails
to a lofty interior crissed with slack phonelines
guy wires and spirals of rope
and the resonant vaults of the hollowed-out word
echoed stupidly,
spilling like amnesia over the signboard
off into an endless etcetera,
AND AND AND, repeated forever.

When I was still easy to amaze
I walked through a field of dead clover
behind a cement plant
and came to a tree full of blackbirds
making a noise like the end of the world.
A city of devils, furious and dead.
Dream-pictures in a crumbling head.
Then they all
(which startled something
asleep in my chest, a memory of some
fledged terror that sprang alive from inside me and
flew) rose
screaming from there and
flew like one shattered thing.

THE FACTS

That fall I crossed over in the back of an open truck
sharing a tarpaulin with a spotted dog, part dingo,
who chewed on the same shoe all the way there.
I sat for ten hours with my back in a tire,
my feet in another tire,
and my head on a box full of gears
while the truck gorged on hundreds of miles
of crumpled up scenery, tracing the phone wires to their source,
counting out miles by the poles
and the road glided up and down like a wave
in a skipping rope through a child's diorama
of tall silos, white steeples
and luxurious slopes polkadotted with cows.

The driver was playing Lou Reed on ten-inch speakers.
I could see a big slice of his face in the side mirror,
mouthing the words. Then there was a long stretch
of nothing, no houses by the road, just mailboxes
with names like Schmidt and McNab
and the driveways so long you could not see
a house at the end. Dogs
taunted us from the ditch,
and we hit some unsavoury roads. The scenery
worsened, the bottlerack spruce stuck right out
like enormous dead weeds. Slovenly black-faced sheep
connived under a tin lean-to. The cattle were thin,
and the driver began swerving to avoid
things that were not there, and in spite of all that
we made very good time. We stopped once
to let the hyena, or dog, or whatever that was,
run wild in a dry creekbed,
And it came back in an hour and a half
dragging a tree.

From there on it was all downhill, the highway flat and slanted
with skid marks arcing into the ditch.
The driver cut the engine and we coasted for hours
with the smell of a forest fire in the air; then we drove
right through the fire, which nobody seemed to be fighting.
The wind was hot and dry, the fire
floated quietly in the branches.
The dog looked at me sideways out of his Egyptian eyes,
the hair behind his ears ruffling in the hot wind.

At last we arrived at the sea. We pushed the truck down a boat launch
into the surf and the engine shattered like crystal,
seawater foaming around it as it sank, the tape-deck blaring.
The driver took off his pants and swung them around his head,
shouting Hoo Eee Ha, then he looked for the hugest rock he could lift
and hurled it into the ocean, bloosh, then another one,
bloosh. I skipped shells on the waves,
the sea chipped them up into a dazzle of sunlight, the dog
ran loose on the beach pulling hundreds of yards
of fish nets and kelp. Boats rose and fell in the bay
like music scaling the rungs of the staff
as the day petered out. That night we made fires on the beach
and swilled cans of pastel-coloured paint
under a frosty-eyed moon.

The next morning, we watched islands forming offshore.
It seems the planet was molten inside and liquefied rock
gushed out of spluttering cracks in the bay.
Tumours of granite bulged up
under shuddering columns of steam, and clouds
goggled over the brim of the sky
like fantastically big shrunken
heads dragging hail over the hump of the world as the rain collapsed
back in the sea, hissing and clattering.

The city was just off the map but not hard to find.
It turned out to be
several towns I'd grown up in
with the street-names confused. I got lost right away
turning left onto Meadowdale, right onto Riverview,
two blocks down Stoneybrook where it meets Mount Pleasant.
Then I came to Pleasantbrook, Meadowview, Stoneymount,
Brookstone and Riverdale, and found myself at a four way stop
near a memorial in mauve granite
reading a long list of names and lifespans,
and they all seemed to be people I knew.
A phone booth was there.
I found my own name five times in the book
at five different addresses, all of them somehow familiar:
Sherwood, Arcadia, Avalon, Canaan, and Grace.
I could see myself living on Grace, but I rented a well-lit room
where King meets Queen overlooking the bridge
and I could see headlights coming on in the grey morning
and taillights riding home in the dark,
and I would listen to the four o'clock traffic report, wondering
if home might be over that bridge
in the dark trees on the far side,
a porchlight in flying snow.

I felt old all that winter
watching powders drift on the ice.
One by one walking corpses of snow
stood up on the rock
to be jabbed in the back by the wind,
herded over the petrified river
into the black trees on the far side.
One vanished, another
rose up behind,
and I'd sit at the window all day,
my eyes shrunk to beebees
my breath stuck fast to the glass,
watching dead things stand up and vanish
in a dimensionless white.

And all night too
with the stars on till four thirty five,
and the city burnt down to coals,
some solitary jesus
with his hands in his pants
moralizing to a bank machine,
the streetlamps untended,
the neon neglected, stove elements
left on in dark kitchens,
and my candle spread out in a cold
blob of wax on a plate,
the wick like a mummified flame,
my breath on the window
and there in the yard by my room
one stiff tree, an elm,
with its roots in the town wiring
pushing its scorched filaments
into the circuitry of the dawn
delaying the sunrise—a vile tree,
knee deep in its own dead leaves,
frazzled and upside down
a mass of congealed lightning
with the bone structure of a horrible dream,
a thick trunk dividing dividing
dividing in a frenzy of mathematics,
littler, skinnier, stingier,
fussing at the frayed hem of the sky,
consumed by its puny uniqueness
like some cipher-crazed maniac
up till dawn counting threads in the drapes,
knowing there's an answer in there,
some number divisible by one and itself,
some code to persuade him it all
made no sense, that the wrong god
was in charge.

I spent hours at the bus stop waiting for nothing,
kicking a stone-hard plum with the toe of my boot,
roadsalt on my eyelashes, the slit-eyed sun
circling the world in freezing rain
like a trapped fox circling the stake,
and there was an immense crumminess all over, the sky
was measly, the city was junk,
the people were cruel. I could say we had all given up
but there was no we, just I's, long subways full of them
flowing into the rain-smudged factories at dawn,
into the steam-windowed kitchens at noon,
into the hydraulics of a revolving dreamworld
after the day. Then after the day
whole personalities were crushed
in the gears of a massive delirium,
the moon screwed into the hospital ceiling
emptying light onto the blinkety blank foreheads,
the eyes swivelling under the lids, the lips
framing each others' names in the dark
dreaming Hello Bruce, dreaming Hello to you too,
dreaming What will he say to me next? Dreaming
my surprise, dreaming his answer, dreaming the air
that I flew through, the battery acid I breathed
and a city that differed in trivial details
from the one where I lived.

Then the sun would climb back on the roofs
rekindle its tired fire, and the day would recur.
I'd rise at five to read Dante in a donut shop, pining for
the romance of a *real* hell, a hell that roared and stank,
a hell of ingenious torments, not this half-baked
hades of sameness where the same morning came back every day,
the same office windows blurry with rain,
lights jittering on,
the coffee maker pissing into a clean pot,
the xerox machine warming up, the wastebaskets empty,
the swivel chair right where it was—how I wished
for a major league hell, but was plagued instead

by one poor fiend with a face like a barbecued apple
who shinnied up my elevator shaft each day
to slide documents under the door for me to sign
and return to sender, please, *without delay*,
Congratulations **Bruce Taylor**, you will receive a fortune
of *one million dollars*. Welcome to riches, **Bruce**,
this is the key to your Rolls,
and sorry seductions like these, no threat
to my soul if I have one, clip out and return
this card to receive
your valuable prize, and that kind of thing.

I found work as a laboratory animal
for a bald man with pinecone sideburns. He tested poisons on me
but I survived them all, he was amazed, we both were,
then I quit that position and nailed a secure job
at the Lady Byng Charity Domicile
stirring vats of grey mush. Eventually I dropped that too
and hammered sheet metal to a school wall;
then I drove a blue van, and later I worked for the city
painting white lines on the roads,
and in the course of that spring
I did every job for a day,
so now I can tell you I've been every person in town
I've done every work that was offered
and lived every life. When I went
I saw myself coming, the trolleys filled up with me
coming and going, the newspaper kept me informed
about all that I did, I looked up
to the rainstreaked windows downtown and saw me
looking down over streets full of me.
A red bird flapped up to its nest, it was me,
she laid me in branches and twine, when I hatched
I asked to be fed, so she brought me
a frantic six-legger and in a snap of the beak
I was gone, mislaid somewhere in a forest of me,
my slim branches clicking and groaning.
I pushed the new leaves from my arms

and they were also me, falling in millions.
I bought books and the author was me
talking to me about me, I was transfixed,
or transported, I searched through the news
clipping out pictures of me for my walls,
and that's when I knew

that my goals lacked focus. I saved up for a truck,
found a good one that summer.
I picked out a sharp-faced dog, half jackal,
lured him to me with a piece of brown meat,
tied him down to the greasy fifth wheel and left town.
I stopped for a sad looking man at the Red Devil Luncheon
kneedeep in dandelions, dressed like a fool,
holding a sign that said Hi, well Hi to you too,
you can ride in the back, ignore the dog, he's been fed,
and then I was off
to ransack the landscape for spots
I could never imagine,
horizons I didn't design,
to find somebody just as he is
in a world that has always been there,
a real world, a big world, a rock-hard world
as wide as all that and made to endure, a well-known world
with the power to pulverize
theories beliefs and conjecture
under the flat rough stones of the facts.

AMERICAN FIREWORKS IN MONTREAL

A summer night, the cooked air
blackens like a fuse.
A double jet trail fades to black.
In the doorway, light is at my back,
coils of steam are rising from my hair.
My murderous neighbour spreads himself a snack
in his yellow kitchen. Everywhere,
music is leaking from the cracks
in peoples' lives, from windows, from car doors.
From my neighbour's house, a muffled war
on channel twelve.
I latch the window and fix tea
in the flickering blue light of his TV.

Tonight there are fireworks. On the quay
along the harbour, in the island park,
half the city gathers in the dark
to witness a controlled catastrophe.
I go too, so does the guy next door,
and half a million of us make our way
to the warehouse village
where a bridge named Jacques Cartier,
looms like a stupendous photostat
in the sky above the charbroiled street,
stepping through homes on steel and granite feet,
big enough to stomp the city flat.

People are roosting in the trees.
They crouch in pylons. I see faces
in the punched-out windows of the factories.
The best spots are already gone.
We infiltrate a scrapyard on our knees
through broken places in a chain-link fence,
and there are hundreds of us scaling an immense
moraine of rusted tricycles and tools.

Around me, disembodied strangers shout
to other strangers. I can just make out
my neighbour's thin, machine-like silhouette
picking its way through wreckage
by the red light of his cigarette.

Darkness thickens over Notre Dame;
a little sunlight seeps
through bandages of cloud
on the bruised horizon. In the crowd
someone says to nobody, aloud,
in a peculiar voice: I don't know where I am.

And now the fireworks. Blam.
A parachute of violet fire
sinks to the river. Blam. A shower
of radioactive seaweed. Blam. Blam. Blam.
A bomb inside a ball in an exploding flower,
sketched against the fountains of Versailles,
with a welder's torch. Cinders fly
in shallow arches, whistling as they die
and trolling incandescent smoke. And then,
expanding and contracting worlds
beaten apart by comets, hurled
from a revolving nautilus; at last,
a kind of writhing Gorgon's-head of light,
scorched on our eyelids. Paralyzed with fright,
we scratch our heads and yawn.
In the darkness, someone shouts: Right on.
Someone answers: U.S.A., *alright.*

In half an hour everyone is gone,
and I'm gone too, paddling my bike through fog.
I lock it to my neighbour's iron grill
and climb upstairs.
The night is very still.
My neighbour's ugly, ladle-footed dog
is whimpering for my neighbour. I can hear it scrape

its animal fingers on the locked screen door.
I spread a blanket on the fire escape
and lie awake on it till four,
then fall asleep. I dream some war
has scrubbed the planet clean, and wake at five
in the blazing vacancy of dawn.
I am the only sentient thing alive
to breathe this freshness. Avalon.
The sky is white. Circles of white
birds hang like brushstrokes on the white
sky; a single jet trail, white,
dissolves to nothing in a wispy "S".
Nothing is emptier, or means less.
Nothing explains this light.

THE ANCESTORS

In which two Explorers become Bridges,
and a Saint is Lightly Browned

At the exact moment when the great
ancestors pass away,
the great names slip from the great
cadavers and the bare idea of Cartier
climbs from its floppy riding boots and meat,
grows an asphalt back and gravel feet
and falls across St. Lawrence, dabbling stone
piles in the unhealthy slime; and lo,
two meaningless immensities are joined.
Their boney geniuses embrace,
like Euclid's perpendiculars.
The two abstractions mesh in space,
with hundreds of other saints and killers
intersecting in the motorways,
which is like watching corpses mate,
the names Cartier, St. Lawrence, St. Justine
coupling in the streets to patriate
the hairy swamps and stippled sand and ducks,
and make this place Quebec. Quebec,
is carried to itself in trucks; the trucks
are hauling pieces of Quebec
across St. Lawrence on Jacques Cartier's neck.

Now open your textbook, please, page one.
A child of Nature, bald and dimpled, stands
contrapposto, languidly baroque,
and blows a graceful fiddlehead of smoke
through a willow-thin tobacco pipe.
An Amerindian, the text explains.
Page two. A pair of wild men dressed in chains
support the family shield of Charles Le Moyne.

Page seven, bottom. Three etched men
in metal shirts and buckled shoes
and bulging pluderhose and plumes
are prancing forward like a troupe
of homicidal dance-instructors, preening
their moustaches as they fall upon
their audience of puzzled Hurons.
That one is Champlain, the caption says.
In fact, it was Champlain himself who drew
all this, recording how he dropped
four pellets in the flared
muzzle of his arquebus (a kind of gun)
and felled three pudgy indigenes with one
fantastic shot. Three of them
are crumpled at his feet.
The rest are faceless, nameless,
naked as a field of wheat,
lifting their cupid's bows to spread
a trellis of arrows over Champlain's head.

Now he is a bridge too, a big one, stretching
from the island to its other shore.
The trucks massage his spine all morning.
In the evening they come back for more.
Below his beamy, buttressed gut
the virulent St. Lawrence carves a rut
from here to the Atlantic. This is what
we boil for coffee, shifting in its crust
of suds and motor oil and rust.

Who was St. Lawrence, you might like to know.
A note on page nineteen supplies a few
important details, some of which are true.
St. Lawrence, it says here, died by barbecue,
raked over coals by some depraved
idolater because his soul was saved,
which theirs were not. And he
is remembered for the most part as

a lively and good-natured victim, one
who made his holy martyrdom look fun.
He let them toast him for a while,
then said, "You'd better turn me, this side's done."
Historical facts are volatile
and must be constantly renewed,
and yet a joke so dazzlingly crude
can never be forgotten.
As long as the fusion-powered sun
goes up and down, and the malignant rivers run
half-toxic to the smouldering sea;
as long as someone innocent remains
for someone who says he's innocent to kill,
we'll have St. Lawrence smiling on the grill,
repeating his last ghastly jest,
"I think I'm ready, folks, eat well."
It doesn't matter if it isn't true.
The truth has vanished. Time won't tell.
The river runs on, the bridge remains.
"Deux hommes sauvages au naturel"
cross it noisily, in chains.

MICROBES

Having learned our enemies are wee,
witless and incapable of spite,
and have no purpose more debased
than to make copies of themselves
and spread these everywhere they can,
their intention being not
to discipline us but just to eat,
propagate and go their way,
we ought to feel a little foolish, like the girl
who thought the party was for her.
Of course, it wasn't a party at all,
a customer had fallen to the floor
and the ambulance was on its way.
The cause of the man's bad luck
was not our perfect author
and his vengeful sprites
but something minuscule that failed inside him,
breaking the fragile fellowship
among his parts.
And it so happens that the enterprising body
and the little mind that tells it where to go
are not one thing, not two,
but a humming municipality of little cells,
soldier cells and doctor cells,
reporter cells and cleaning woman cells,
and even a small uprising
in the least valued organ,
miles from the priceless heart,
imperils all.
Your blood has no idea who you are,
your membranes have intentions of their own.
The whole dazzled colony goes walking
into the dispersion of its life
shapely and upright, like a swarm of bees.

X-RAY

Who is that walking on the sun?
Me in my white hot bones
modelled in interstellar fuzz,
a guest from the dead channel.
Me as a radiant marionette
jumbled on the firelit wall
in the humming ossuary. All
this came from in there, words
packed in those cocoons of floss
inside the charred geode
of its skull. What you see
here belongs to me, is me
without the hidden thread
that strings the cannibal
necklace of its spine
to the grinning trophy of the head.
But what makes roger jolly
is the hope that he
will get to the end of his work
and climb out free
in the splintered light
to enjoy a good joke
and not be absorbed
in the mush of time
but persist for centuries
caked in hot sediments
between a forked stick
a flake of white rock and a shell,
and not be a ghost, a vaporized human,
a bad feeling at large,
but his own strict self
staying on to discredit the lie
that life, all life,
is one shivering tender
mass that throbs and quails

under the harsh light
of the facts. That all things
are liquefied at death and run
into the same shimmering pool.
That everything alive is one
sweet-tempered creature
mangled in the spokes of the sun.

BUS STATION

Kids are doing things they're not supposed to.
Sweethearts take the escalator up.
A man with too much hair is getting close to
something in a polystyrene cup.

How painfully that lady walks,
and how oblivious to what she wears.
Somehow she finds the row of chairs
where Television blooms on stalks.

She feeds a coin to one and stares.
Is it a fact that everybody longs
to do things nobody discusses?
Go, people. Ride away from here in buses.

MY SON

How much death in this small fist?
How much in twelve weeks of the summer,

in the black star-map of his footprint
pinned to the wall above my desk?

Fourteen pounds: I have a bag of rice
heavier than that.

Yesterday he fell, or I dropped him
three steps down to a slab of concrete.

I examined him well, he was still closed
and perfect all over,
not open at all. Nothing was different
but still I saw it,
how much death there was,
how all of it poured out, a cloud of moths
hiding the light.

SPRING

The first banjo chords of spring after that endless
fugue on the hydraulic organ.
Dogs are running with their leashes off.
A skinny man
has dismantled his motorcycle in the sun.
A child is not wearing mitts.
It's my child
with a plastic shovel,
pushing some carbonized snow
over the curb.

Someone I know well is down in his basement
going through boxes.
He is sitting in a big pile of letters,
yearbooks, notepads,
figure drawings in orange conté,
things he has kept in case.

Nobody can say how he ended up here
with these boxes
and the whir of the gas furnace,
the faint, faraway sound
of children shrieking.

It is this sound
that he is listening to, and
I recognize the look
on his face, I've seen it before—
a focussed grief, no
puzzlement, no
I've seen it before, oh yes
on a child trying to reattach
a doll's arm.

GARDEN OF PARALLAX, MOUNT ROYAL CEMETERY

1

They were moved here in boxes
and stored under the field
between the small fruit trees.
The treasures, the treasures.
Put there for safe-keeping,
folded in burgundy cloth,
the spot carefully marked
as if someone had said to herself,
placing these here,
we'll come back for them soon.

2

One day a regatta of white and blue cars
swayed up the gravel path, stopping to let out
five women in soft cardigans
and full skirts
their white hair under control in the breeze.

From some distance off in the heat,
the sound of car doors slamming shut.

3

When you take this path,
you are shadowed by names.
This is the garden of parallax.
The stones drift along in a daze,
converging and sliding apart,

CAMPBELL O'MALLEY MADRID

WALLINGFORD ROBIDOUX SMALL

4
Someone has been making space
for new plots, clearing room
on the side of a hill.

The new sod is rumpled like blankets,
the old sod rises in piles
at the edge of the field.

The huge orange backhoe, asleep in the sun
has black vinyl seats
patched with white tape and hot
to the touch.

Saplings tilt in the back of a truck,
more than a dozen, their roots
swaddled in burlap.

5
A horrid sight:
red ribbons fluttering on
shrivelled carnations.
The black puzzle of a flower
still in its pot,
rustling when the wind picks up.

This is what they used to call
a zephyr, a good wind
from the west. A Zephyr.

6
When they do come back
with handspades and rakes
it is not to unearth their lost lovers
but to be with the hard-working birds on a Sunday,
helping things grow.

WHY I WORK

I've seen movie stars disappear under quicksand,
the cool muck closing over the crown of the head.
Today, that would be a pleasure.
I'm sunk to the collar in camel-brown pillows
in the full heat of summer, fanning the walls with my gills.
The fat moist lips of the couch
sip coins from my pockets
and I don't care, my eye
climbs into the fridge
and closes the door,
the couch steals my keys, I don't care,
it can have what it needs
my pencil, my wallet, my arms
are draped on my belly
like two wrong ends of a seatbelt,
impossible to connect them, pointless to try.
I might just lie here
till somebody throws me away,
or mildew consumes me, or flies, or the couch,
but a minute goes by
and something pitiful, weak and inside me,
a spiteful voice
says: dance. And I do.
I am hauled to my feet
and the minuscule voice knocks me around the room
kicking like a pithed frog.

IDLENESS

Drawing a treble clef
on the wall with my eye,

squinting at a chandelier
till each bulb in its red fez sprouts
vibrating bristles,

counting flies in a museum cafeteria
next to a table
where two lovers are coming apart
with a long talk and whole minutes
of horrified silence:
they are doing this terrible thing,
unwrapping their sadness
and showing it
to one another.
It is so awful how their voices
tremble,
but notice
the idleness of their hands
stacking coins,
pushing crumbs with a bank card,
breaking chunks from the rim
of a disposable cup
and placing these inside the cup until
there isn't a cup to contain them,
just a small pile of styrofoam chips.

ERRATA

Diners are asked to please imagine more
onions in the salad, and less salt.

On page 5, for
"his ram around her" read
"his arm." His arm around her.

Put the ram out of your thoughts.
Put him nowhere; put her arm
around him, knot her hands
into the fleece, drop
the flint axe of his head into the folds
of her blouse, place her cool
palm on the defective spiral
of the horn—sequester both

in the mistakescape of your memory
under a tree which God didn't make
by a river which is always
the same river twice.

See rain climb the backdrop, inverted canyons
towering over, all crags
and crescendos. And in the east

the jumbled icosahedrons
crossed beams and cockeyed spires
of a town called Amsteradm,
irradiating a pure confused particularity
over the crisp horizon,
sharp and detailed as a jigsaw puzzle.

A bird calls out in Latin
from the singed grass.

Ink in the stream
scribbles the tablature to symphonies of noise.

Inventors ply the weird air
in rattling anachronisms, boys

hiss softly under the ovoid moon:
you are my read one, I am oyurs

in the evening, a dead hedge
rattles, it is made of words

the shadow of a tree swims over the sidewalk,
words, words, words

the evening takes us apart
atom by atom, untying the laces,

salting us into the halflight speck by
fleck, and we float off on a puff of talcum
to the strains of Bach's air
on a G string played in the key of A.

ENGLISH LESSONS

Thank you, but the meat you sell is old.
The male in that establishment is thin.
A cross-eyed girl is living in the stairwell.
Marilyn suggests we take her in.

Dad controlled our lives for years;
his ghost plays yahtzee in the upstairs room.
I warned you not to ridicule the bears.
The bride-to-be is sweeping with the broom.

Her hiccups came and went away like that.
Your so-called statue takes up too much space.
Forgive me, but this dinner is a rat.
The thing you thought was lovely was my face.

TV

Sometimes it seems to believe I am somebody else,
someone who wants to see strangers
wipe out in huge waves,
golden-haired dogs catching frisbees,
cars being lifted with gigantic magnets.

Sometimes it almost seems to know me, it shows
a hillside in China,
the pope in his street clothes,
the eyes of a rapist.

It is trying to be funny and all it wants in return
is some of my time,
which is fine, I don't think
I would have spent the day reading Aquinas
or putting up dry-wall.

Look, a lot of good teeth.
An interesting bulge.

There's quite a lot there if you know where to look.
A man with his jacket on fire,
a palm tree bending over, a heart
pumping in the surgeon's hand.

I have a feeling I've been here before.
None of it seems new.
But I seem to be dying just as quickly
no matter what I do.

Aha, the dog can open a cage with his mouth.
That woman is setting them straight.
Cars are flying overhead in slow motion.

The same things happen here
as anywhere. People break down
in hospital corridors.
Train bridges collapse.
A desperate man burns down his own barn.

A wasp hugs a paralyzed cutworm.

A corn-poppy nods in a field
of unfocussed grass.

Agate-coloured spheres circle noiselessly
among wakeful stars.

A professor walks through ruins
while cleaning his glasses.

A scowling officer with a patch over one eye
parts the slats of a blind.

Mysterious boxes are unloaded.

Flies settle on a child dying in a pile of garbage.

A young man explains how to wax skis.

Oh no, it is wasting my time!
I am forgetting to harvest the pumpkins,
the pumpkins are rotting in the field.
The animals haven't been fed.
I have forgotten to sleep
and am spending my night watching people I don't know
pretend to be people I don't know.
It isn't real.

But what did I ever get out of being
real? You run a huge risk in the world.
If you walk there, you will die.

If you eat that, you will die.
If you stand under those, you will die.

But here in the shared light
I can die every minute
and stand up again, yawning and stretching.

Here, the future
is practised until it is perfect.
The past is preserved
until it is needed, and I,
I am killing time without mercy
to the sound of bodiless laughter
ghostly orchestras
and frantic applause.

ORANGUTANS

We have come here for the peanuts and to meet
the mortified stares of the wild men,
quarantined on their island of packed dirt,
in their crater of painted cement
under the theatrical fork
of a plaster tree.

We have entrusted them with three tires,
a bundle of rope
and as much straw as they can use,

and with a little encouragement
they have manufactured
minute quantities of fun,
twirling a stem of clover,
patting a small pile of dust,
pouring sand over a beetle.

We have also built bleachers for ourselves
to make sure we are comfortable while we wait
for the interesting thoughts
we are planning to have
as we watch what the orangutans
do.

"TALK NOT CHEAP" SAYS MONTREAL POET, 35

1.

It is not just that a live fish
is a luxury, but a dead one
joins the economy.

Last year, the economy pumped iron.
The wheat fields gleamed like brocade on an admiral's arm.
The tomatoes were redder than ever, the farm
was on steroids, our eggs
weighed half a pound each: something

was working. Somebody
cut meat and apportioned the water
and metred the air in our throats.

The gauges flickered, the talk was clocked,
the poets were paid by the word. But words

do not always come cheap,
we can't always afford them. This year
we are shrinking, things won't
get described, which doesn't kill them.
Most things go years without
being described
and it doesn't kill them.

Soon things will pick up,
the economy
will stagger back from the crypt,
parting the dirt
with its black fingers,
shaking the mould from its flab,
and each time it returns it is more, more
bloated and hairy and strong than before
and more certain to get what there is,

if there's anything left.

So next year, the words are in short supply
and if we need to, we coin new ones.

Here are next year's words:

cihuj, azghz, fma
kykykyma, ooooo

get used to them.

2.

Advice to winners (pin this
to your keyboard):

if you want to obliterate something,
advertise it.

I'm just old enough to remember
Love Love on the radio,
and Love on the cover of Time.

This year
it was The Environment.
For ten dollars and tax
you can have the smoking remains of the world
printed on a shirt.

And if you say "We love this planet"
someone is certain to ask,
can we afford it?

3.

It's not just that we can do without
environments; the truth is,
we hate this one.

We could just punch that hill,
extinguish the stupid dirt,
catch all the muskrats
and snap off their fucking heads.
Kick over the trees like chairs,
hack them all up to make chairs
to fill up our buildings with chairs
so we have somewhere to sit
while we plot our next move.
And you know well enough what that
will be, everyone knows that we can
and we will too, anywhere we want,
anytime.

And when we've used it all up
we won't go slithering back to the past.
We will wait.
We will wait for a plough
that can till the cement,
a hen that eats oil,
a new kind of child
powered by shimmering ooze,
an infant superhuman man with horns and a halo
and diesel smoke whistling from his noseholes
and a tag saying hallelujah tied to his tongue.
A clever child with ideas
for improving reality by increments,
superb suggestions, seeping like oil into a hinge,
dissolving confusion and surprise with unique
preparations.
Everyone is sucked right in.
The fish are sucked into the turbines
the birds are sucked into the jets
the dotted white lines
are sucked under the car,
the future is sucked into the present
and sprayed into the past, and the past
is just there all the time.

They used to sing this on the radio:
Canada, we love you.
But any day now there won't be
a Canada-shaped thought in the mind
or Canada-sounding words for that song

but there will be Canada money in my pants
and Canada trees for the forklift
and Canada gas for the car,

and everything will have that familiar strangeness.

From here,
I can see the future,
there, on the third shelf from the bottom
still in its original box, packed in styrofoam pellets,
giving off that factory-new smell.

MOON TOWN

Life is short, but afternoons are long.
Adrift in the vastness of
a tuesday, I used to put my cheek
up to the perforated hardboard
behind the TV to feel its heat,
looking in at the red vitals
of our modernity, and I knew that we
were in training for a strange
future, for lives filled with
dial gauges and horseshoe magnets,
moon towns and mechanical pets.
And it has been strange,
but one thing has never changed, I still
look into the future
closely inspecting the days left,
staring at them until they grow transparent,
like the blades of a fan.

4646 HUTCHISON ST.

To Robyn

I used to come here, when invited
and sit at a pink table, talking too fast.
Now I live here.
Those are my avocados on the sill.

I'm finding out things you would have known:
that you have to kick the summer kitchen door,
that the hot water pipe plays sousaphone;
where the squeaks are in the floor,
and how to map a trail
from the bedroom to the fridge
without catching your socks on a nail.

This place gathers time by the armful,
hoards dust in its nail-holes,
mulls on the contents of its boxes.
Greenery brushes the window, the sun comes
at three fifteen and stays
till three twenty.

Walking in sock feet
on the cold basement floor,
climbing the stairs with a basket of damp
clothes, turning off the light
with an elbow, shutting the door with a foot —
this might have been you.

Nothing changes for a while.

Water goes around and around
in the walls.

Then something happens, the door,

the door is wide open,
there is wind in the kitchen
whirling on the red tile floor.
Outside on the line the clothes
do an arabian dance
rippling and shimmying and
making a fool out of everyone in broad daylight.

SUNDAY

The faithful still poking around
on that petrified hulk,
surprised every sunday to find
the church in its place,
sunk to the haunches in rock
and red weeds. And who can say there is not
some meek little god up there
in the rafters,
some sluggish, detached
abstract and disinterested
cordial, immortal guy
curled up on a twig of the world tree—

some slow-thinking everlaster
to whom the threnody of life
is a brisk hornpipe played on a penny flute,

to whom the pageant of days
is a strobe light on black cloth,
mountains cresting and crashing like surf,
matterhorns and gibraltars,
and whole continents wafting like smoke
over the vibrating blue.

To him, I suppose,
to someone like him,
the stores on my street
would flicker and shift
like flats in a silent film
where the pixillated
pedestrians trot
up through the decades
and down in one brand new
old-fashioned hat
after another,

bristling with dead fashions,
feathers and stoles—
a jittering gauze
on which the shadows dash,
waltzing their moist lovers.

To a durable god our slow
chant of longing and moans of regret
are a creek trebling
over the cool stones,
the buzzing of flies
as he reclines in his days without end,
the summer grass damp on his back.

VOCAL ACCOMPANIMENT

Thou need'st not ask of me
What this strong music in the soul may be!
—Samuel Taylor Coleridge

A melody is stuck in my head, a bad one,
some kind of deranged
circus tune played on a
steam-powered Symphonotron,
and it is making a mockery of my dejection.
The poets, the old ones, grievers of yore,
had better music
for their dolor, lacrimations
for the violon d'amore,
koto solos, billowing chorales,
whereas I feel awful to the tune of
mouth harps, glass flutes and
hawaiian guitars.
It is not a dark night but a frenzied
hootenanny of the soul.
On the rolling boards
balloonoid sailors and their spindly gals
clobber stubble-chinned buffoons
with rubbery mallets.
"Reality's dark dream," as Coleridge called it
in the calcine deeps of his despair
seems horribly bright now,
big on the skins of the eye,
while the mind's ears are flapping in time to
asthmatic concertinas
and the shrill peening of steel drums.

LIGHT

A complicated thought
striking the forehead, clink,
and glancing off it at an angle.
Roomlight garbled in a drink,
dashed to fractions on a tile
or looped in a fluourescent tangle
underneath the pool.

Tonight, a neighbour's house on fire
makes enough light to write this by.
Tomorrow, I'll admire the sky
through the lathing in his walls,
and say, "The light, the light that falls
through Caldwell's ceiling
warms a peculiar-looking cat."

PALAIS DE JUSTICE

They are here to be dealt with
on a weekday morning,
when the unemployed are still
climbing into their housecoats, and the employed
are opening their mail.
In the malls the steel grills are unrolling,
the new weather is on its way,
but here, instead of climbing on fire escapes
and pissing in phone booths,
the criminals wait for hours on plastic chairs
in a well-lit hall.
They have messy hair and tattoos,
and ought to be locked up,
but how obedient they are,
waiting their turn,
clutching the papers they were told to bring.
One is walking up and down,
tapping his thigh with a brochure,
his sneakers chirping on the marble floor.
Another is pulling hairs
from the back of his hand.

Something amazing is happening behind those doors.
Innocence is throttling guilt,
the jury is clacking its mouth-parts,
experts have wrapped a helpless man with silk.

But out here, the staff
are having a day on the job.
The law passes back and forth over our heads
like a xerox light, and everyone is led
to other rooms where they will stand in line
to sign whatever they are told to sign.

JAIL

I have a jail in mind,
I call it "jail,"
as in "He went to jail,"
and I put all my prisoners
there, shoeless, beltless,
eking light from a slot in the wall,
collecting rain
in a dish, sniffing the rain.
Prisoners of all kinds and times.

I was once in a Turkish town, too small
to show up on a map, too flat
to be seen from the road, too pale
to appear on the dust, lost in the yellowy grass
and the receding trees, where the goats
soaked their beards in a Byzantine sarcophagus
and no one built anything new.
The power came in on one wire,
the news sifted down from above,
the soft drinks rode to town once a month
in the back of a van.

It was here that we toured the town jail
and met the young cops in their olive-green pants,
the officers anxious to prove they were not
torturers. Look, they said,

no clump of hair on the walls;
no word scratched with a spoon;
no stain on the floor
(but a well-scrubbed place where the drain
puckered into the concrete)

the mattress pristine
the washbasin, crooked but clean—

a room where the day
was steel-wooled and chloroxed away
during the night
and the next morning the door
would open again, to receive
casual visitors.
And what a door,
enough enamelled steel
to blunt a tank,
yet rippled like the side of a tent,
and the ceiling painted, of all colours,
blue, sky blue.

They asked us questions.
"Do you not have jails in Canada?" We do.
"Do your jails have locks?" Oh yes.
"Are the inmates delighted to be there?" No.
"My friend, I can see
that you and I are very much alike."
And I told him that could be true.
"And we are every bit as *good* as you."
And with that, I emphatically agree.
"And what is more the so-called Armenian genocide
is a terrible lie."

And I meant to disagree,
but just then they served us "cay,"
which is their word for tea,
in little bell-shaped glasses.

We tinkled the cube sugar
with miniature spoons.
"We grow this here," he said,
"on the coast of the blue Black Sea
where it is always cool."
And I can picture the tea gardens.
I have never been there,
but I have seen the postcards.

INHUMAN WISHES

from Juvenal's 10th Satire

Wherever you go, from Mexico to Madagascar,
everyone ignores the facts,
and nobody remembers how to pray.
God, as you know, has his ways.
He might smash up your house for no reason,
or roll burning rocks down your street.
But he'd just as soon *not*.
So, with the right prayer
perhaps you could turn things around.
Well at least you could try.
But what can you safely request?
You may count on one thing: whatever you choose
it will injure us all in the end.

It is always the same, when they get their three wishes.
The thug turns his gun on himself,
the senator chokes on his tongue
the millionaire just disappears
in a puddle of fat.

So what must you pray for? Fame
is attractive, that is,
attracts bullets. The same goes for power,
and money, well money is worse.
Look how it clogs the vaults,
how low the money-barge
rides in the water, sunk to the rails under
gold, green paper and credit notes.
Well, rich individuals die
just as unpleasantly as you or I,
and in the meantime they are worried that we
will help ourselves
to some of what they have,

64

that we'll jump them in some poorly lit arcade
and make off with their bundles of loot.
Yet what is the first request
at every wishing well?
Unbounded wealth, or something
along those lines.

Let me tell you, though, you won't drink cyanide
from a dixie cup; your dose will be served
in crystal stemware
from a flask of blown Venetian glass.
That's just how it is. Get rich, and every sip
might be poisoned by some
fortune-hunter, or your envious aunt.
So reserve a good word for the old cranks,
poets and pedagogues, Juvenal, Johnson and Swift,
who lived among scoundrels and bank presidents
and still could manage a caustic laugh.

They in their time saw things
to make them shiver with disgust,
and yet *they* never saw a hotel doorman
dressed like the holy pontiff
prance up to a long white car
to liberate some thickset chieftain of trade
and his diamond-encrusted mistress
teetering under a twelve pound hat.
They never saw dog psychiatry and mail order brides
and nose surgery on national TV
The ancients missed out on all that,
yet they never ran short of
sinister fools to deride.
They stood quite tall
in a landscape thick with buffoons
mocking them all to little bits.

So why do we pray for trash?
God breaks his back

lifting new delights into the world each day,
hoisting the sun over the hill,
hurling the planets through the cosmos,
levitating the grain,
all for our pleasure, and we ask for toys!

People are often done in by power,
when they have it. Bent over with medals,
their chins drag on the pavement.
But soon their statues come down,
they are scrapped or melted.
Remember Lenin, hear the roar of the smelter
liquefying his face, his bronze beard,
his long coat and accusing finger.
He was poured back into the mould
to be rehabilitated as ashtrays,
scale replicas of classic cars,
portrait busts of J.F.K. Does anyone mind?
Last year's leader is struck from the money
and this year's face
is all over the walls.
Each of them, each in his time
will be dragged through the schools by the heels,
pressed flat in the textbooks,
hung up to dry in the halls.
Careful professors will measure their organs,
poking and joking. The students will snore.

Schwarzkopf too, in his triumph.
He bobbed on the airwaves like a bathtoy;
he swam the channels, his name
was etched on the air.
But when the oil-smoke cleared
what was left of the General,
his dappled pants, his shiny cheeks?
He had his tickertape parade.
Then it was talk shows and quiz shows, and finally
whatever happened to Stormin' Whatsisname,

and where is he now?
A puzzled ghost rereading
his ghostwritten memoirs.

May he live to die well—most don't.
Few national saviours end in respectable ways.
As a rule they survive long enough
to be airlifted out of the mob's hands,
and beg for asylum in a friendly state
where the weather is nice.
But supposing the hero survives?
Well, he dies anyway.
Take Stalin—dig him up if you have to,
pour his remains on the scales:
how much does *he* weigh?
There is the famous man, that's him.
He said "bomb," and the missiles
rose from their holes in the ground;
he said "world," and the world
changed shape.
And what has he come to?
a handful of stories,
a few rolls of black and white film,
a halloween mask in a joke-shop window.

There once was man named Hughes,
and one world was too little for him.
He slid down its walls
like a rat in a bathtub,
and yet in the end
a couple of billion dollars was just enough
to bury his carcass
under a mountain of expensive stuff;
he burrowed down in his pile of cash
and lay there till he rotted right away.
He died horribly one day
(well who doesn't die?) and nobody cared, not one
of the million workers he could buy and sell

with a jab of the pen. Well, well.
How much does Hughes own now?
His property's a bit reduced:
a couple of yards of yellow dirt.
Not even that: a puff of dust,
some mud on your sneakers, a few
minerals in your spring water.

So by all means, make me rich, good God,
and while you're at it
make me immortal,
or at least let me live to be old, old, old.
Let me outlast my friends,
let all the deceased losers
live to envy my long long life. Let them
resent me for a change.

But what can we say for old age?
If you're lucky, your mind remains sound—
sound enough to savour your losses
and feel the impending decline.
Food somehow loses its taste, and your wine
might be cough syrup for all you care.
I trust you will enjoy watching your hair
slide away and your cheeks
crumple like overcooked eggplant.

And I suppose you'll remember that appetites endure
when the means to fulfill them are gone.
You will dream about steak
as you sip yellow mush through a tube,
wheedling like a baby bird.
Or you'll pay some good-looking youngster
to finger your lank noodle
in a room with no air.

If your luck fails, your mind goes first.
You retain just enough of your judgement

to be certain the children have poisoned your food,
or to imagine the radio
is really a bomb
and the year is nineteen-seventy-two,
Or to alter your will,
leaving your ill-gotten hoard
to the kindly young man
who controls your investments.
Or you survive just sufficiently long
to wish you had not, who knows?

But I see you're too clever,
you'll pray for good health
to go with your infinite years.
Fine then, live
to bury your children.
Stay smooth and well-built
while your sweetheart grows
lumpy and tough as a ginger root,
slipping away, in the natural course,
into the welcoming night
leaving you to your solitude
and your funerals.

Is there anything left to pray for then? Well,
no. If you want my opinion,
let God do as he pleases.
He loves you approximately as well
as you love yourself.
But if you have to waste your sundays
begging for help, then pray
for a soul that can know it must die
and not be paralyzed with fear.
Pray for the courage to endure the worst.
Pray for a supple and respectful mind.

But these are things that you already have.

WHAT CAN YOU DO

How does a girl in red buckled slippers
turn into this hard-mouthed employee
with opinions on foreigners?

What made an agile child
grow way too big
and accustomed to living with cats?
Why should a young woman say (before
she is twenty!) "well, that's life," and
"what can you do?"

What she did do
was fill her apartment with
saddle chairs and bentwood dinettes.
Then she frowned until a letter 'I'
between inverted commas
was notched into her forehead.

Possibly she once thought
she might live in the woods;
that a man with no shirt
would be poking her cheek with a straw, she
lithe in her socks,
whiter than percale and smelling of lemons,
he with an armload of cattails,
a curly-haired dog,
blue jeans and thongs, an adorable stammer,
she with a walkman on, singing too loudly,
he with a belt made of knotted bandannas,
she with a skirt she's picked up secondhand.

Nobody hopes to live seven floors up,
to memorize jokes,
to lean over the cards with a fresh pack of smokes
and take some kind of greedy
delight in the frog-headed truth,

saying "O.K., I had plans,
but they were smushed on the milestones,
drowned under millstones,
sniggered at by selfish men.
What can you do?"

Last year in my little yard there was an iris
that never became
what the catalog said it should be,
a delicately ruffled picotee
with a gash of maroon in its beard,
abundant bloom, an orderly habit of growth,
a mulish stamina and serene
indifference to the common pests.
Well, nobody cut off its head with a frisbee
or poured caustic lime on its roots,
yet none of the flowers came true.
It looked like its skin was too tough.
The flower just matured in its calyx,
ripened, then shrivelled away in the dark
without ever
twirling about in cranberry-coloured velour,
flouncing its pleats or having
a night to remember.

I paid a surprising amount for the rhizomes,
but what can you do?

The best you can do might be nothing.
A girl in red buckled slippers
could keep that up for decades until
she has become truly old and has lost
what we think of as the human shape,
at which time for reasons unknown her loveliness
is returned to her
and she sits in a purplish sweater, smoking,
a small wind lifting the fringe of her scarf,
in the day's heart

in a small city garden
where a few irises flourish, crimson sateen,
crushed gold, a few
jonquils in frothy camisoles, a few
monkish ground-dwelling birds
playing ocarinas in the sandlots.
The sky growing wider, the spring soil
rumpled like clothes at the foot of a bed
in which soft little creatures are mating.

LOVELY

The past is lovely, it lasts forever.
Somewhere, I'm still
lying under the lawn sprinkler
with no coppertone on,
the grass cool and elastic under my back,
a black spaniel nuzzling my feet.
The cars are old-fashioned and optimistic,
the people who drive them
have fallen in love with the future.
They can't know that when they get here
they will love the past more,
that the present will look like
a stupendous machine
for forcing things to stop existing.
Well, to live for the moment
is best, but the moments, the little
jiffies, they are startled
to be here, like
the high-shouldered cuprous beetles
that live beneath patio stones,
if you're curious you lift one up
and let it run down your arm.
The other ones scoot for cover,
struggling down into the leaf mulch,
kicking frantically.

SPOOK

There are things so close to you
they are amazing—something alien
in the back of your hand,
a wildness in your child's eyes.

Once I received a package in the mail
containing my own shoes.

Then, travelling on a bus at night
I spent a long time looking
at water drops branching on the window,
my huge spook moving
over miles of dark,
its eyes inscrutable.

ERYTHRONIUM

I can never remember what the word "crepuscular" means, although I've looked it up a hundred times. I have heard about a man worse off than that. He was unable to have new memories at all. He could not learn a name or a face. A minute would pass and the friend was a stranger again, the old joke became funny. He kept finding out that his dear wife had died. Again and again, a grief that would never be old.

I would love to memorize the names of the fish and the birds. Last summer I learned the herbaceous perennials that grow in my town, and for a while I had them by heart. Then winter came and the foliage went under snow. By spring some things I knew well had gone off into the strangeness, seeping away into my quiet house while I napped. A few days ago, I found myself mute before a flower I knew, a yellow one shaped like a pagoda.

The word "crepuscular" means "living in twilight." I find myself drifting along in this twilight, a small wind drying my eyes. I am holding a feather, which I must have found on the street back there. The neighbourhood is full of locked cars and half-naked children playing under streetlights. Two of the children are mine. Hosewater patters softly on the bricks. Shapes I don't recognize are coming toward me out of the twilight, waving as if they know me well.